The Complete Guide to Understanding Dementia for Beginners

Symptoms, Care Strategies, and Resources

CLARA JENNINGS

Table of Contents

Introduction 1

Designed for You: Clear, Simple, and Accessible 2

The Purpose of This Book 3

Chapter One 5

Understanding Dementia – The Basics 5

Common Misconceptions About Dementia 6

How Dementia Affects the Brain and Body 8

Types of Dementia 9

Chapter 2 11

Recognizing the Early Signs and Taking Action 11

Chapter 3 17

Types of Dementia 17

Chapter 4 21

Understanding Risk Factors and Preventive Measures 21

Chapter 5 27

The Stages of Dementia – What to Expect 27

Chapter 6 31

The D.I.C.E. Approach – 31

Managing Behavioral Changes 31

Chapter 7 35

Care and Treatment Options 35

Making Informed Decisions 35

Chapter 8 41

Taking Care of the Caregiver – You Matter Too 41

Practical Tips for Taking Care of Yourself 41

Finding Support 42
Taking Care of Your Health 43
Balancing Caregiving and Self-Care 44
You Matter Too 44
Chapter 9 45
Navigating Legal and Financial Challenges 45
Chapter 10 51
Emotional Support and Communication for Families 51
Maintaining Communication 51
Preserving Dignity and Connection 52
Talking to Children About Dementia 53
Sharing Responsibilities and Seeking Support 54
A Family's Journey 55
Chapter 11 57
Resources and Support Networks 57
Finding Supportive Organizations 57
Joining Support Groups 59
Using Technology for Support 60
Building a Support Network 61
Staying Informed and Engaged 62
You Are Not Alone 63
Conclusion 65

Introduction

Dementia is more than just forgetfulness or occasional confusion. It is a condition that changes how the brain works, affecting memory, thinking, and behavior. These changes make daily life harder, not only for the person experiencing them but also for their family and friends.

Understanding dementia is important because it helps us face the challenges it brings. When we know what dementia is and how it affects people, we can respond with patience, kindness, and practical support. Whether you are a family member, a friend, or a caregiver, this knowledge empowers you to make a positive difference.

Dementia isn't just one illness. It's a term that covers different conditions like Alzheimer's disease, vascular dementia, and others. Each type affects the brain in its own way. By learning about these differences, you can better understand what your loved one is going through and how to help them.

As dementia progresses, its effects become more noticeable. Small memory lapses may grow into significant memory loss. Tasks that were once simple might become difficult. These changes can be scary and confusing. But by knowing what to expect, you can face these moments with understanding rather than fear.

When your loved one forgets things or repeats questions, it's the illness affecting their brain. Remembering this helps you respond with compassion. Understanding removes some of the frustration and allows for more meaningful connections.

There are many myths about dementia. Some people think it's just a normal part of getting older, but that's not true. Dementia causes serious changes that go beyond typical aging. Recognizing the signs early can lead to better care and planning for the future.

Every person's experience with dementia is unique. Some may struggle with memory, while others find it hard to speak or move. By understanding these differences, you can provide the specific support your loved one needs. This knowledge helps you be there for them in the best possible way.

Designed for You: Clear, Simple, and Accessible

Facing dementia can feel overwhelming, especially with complicated medical terms thrown around. This book is written just for you—someone who wants clear and simple information without all the jargon.

Think of this book as a friendly guide. We'll talk about dementia in plain language that makes sense. You won't need a medical degree to understand the topics we cover. Our goal is to make the information easy to read and use in your daily life.

We know that medical words can be confusing. Words like "**cognitive decline**" or "**neurons**" might not mean much to you. That's why we've avoided them here. Instead, we focus on what you need to know in a way that's straightforward and helpful.

The Purpose of This Book

This book is here to help you through every step of caring for someone with dementia. We offer practical tips and emotional support because both are important on this journey.

You'll find real-life advice on how to communicate better, handle daily routines, and deal with challenging behaviors. Whether it's changing things at home to make it safer or finding new ways to connect with your loved one, we've got you covered with ideas that work.

Caring for someone with dementia can be tough on your feelings too. It's hard to see someone you care about change in unexpected ways. That's why we also focus on supporting you. We'll share ways to cope with stress, take care of yourself, and find moments of joy along the way.

This journey is not just about managing a condition; it's about keeping the bond strong between you and your loved one. Even when things get hard, there are still opportunities for love, laughter, and connection. We're here to help you find those moments and cherish them.

Chapter One

Understanding Dementia – The Basics

What Is Dementia?

Dementia is a condition that affects how the brain works. It makes it hard for people to remember things, think clearly, and make decisions. This is more than just normal forgetfulness that happens as we age. Dementia can change a person's daily life in many ways.

It's important to know that dementia is not one single disease. It is a term used for different problems that affect the brain. Alzheimer's disease is one type of dementia, but there are others like vascular dementia and Lewy body dementia. Each type affects people differently.

People with dementia may forget recent events or familiar tasks. They might lose things often or have trouble following a conversation. As time goes on, they may struggle with simple activities like cooking or paying bills. They might also feel confused about where they are or what time it is.

Everyone experiences dementia differently. Some people might have more trouble with memory, while others might find it hard to speak or move. Understanding these differences helps us support our loved ones better.

Even though dementia gets worse over time, people living with it can still enjoy happy moments. With care and understanding, we can help them feel valued and maintain their dignity.

Common Misconceptions About Dementia

There are many misunderstandings about dementia. Let's clear up some of the common myths.

Myth 1: Dementia Is a Normal Part of Aging

Many people think everyone gets dementia if they live long enough. This is not true. While it's more common in older adults, many people grow old without any serious memory problems. Forgetting a name now and then is normal. Forgetting the names of close family members might be a sign of dementia.

Myth 2: Dementia Only Affects Memory

Dementia does affect memory, but it also affects other things. People might have trouble speaking, understanding others, or solving simple problems. Some might find it hard to move around or keep their balance.

Myth 3: There's Nothing You Can Do Once Diagnosed

While there is no cure for dementia, there are ways to help manage it. Doctors can offer treatments that may slow down symptoms. Early diagnosis allows families to plan and find support services.

Myth 4: All Types of Dementia Are the Same

There are different types of dementia, each with its own symptoms. Knowing the type can help in finding the best care. For example, Alzheimer's disease often starts with memory loss, while vascular dementia might affect planning and thinking skills.

Myth 5: Dementia Develops Suddenly

Dementia usually develops slowly over time. Early signs can be easy to miss. Recognizing them early can help in managing the condition better.

Myth 6: People with Dementia Can't Enjoy Life

People with dementia can still find joy in activities they love. They might enjoy music, spending time with family, or hobbies. Focusing on what they can do helps improve their quality of life.

Myth 7: Only Older People Get Dementia

While dementia is more common in older adults, younger people can get it too. This is called early-onset dementia and can happen to people in their 40s or 50s.

Myth 8: People with Dementia Can't Make Decisions

In the early stages, many people with dementia can still make choices about their lives. It's important to include them in decisions for as long as possible.

Myth 9: Dementia Is Always Inherited

Having a family member with dementia might increase the risk, but it doesn't mean a person will definitely get it. Healthy habits like eating well and staying active can help lower the risk.

How Dementia Affects the Brain and Body

Dementia changes how the brain works. The brain has different parts that control memory, speech, movement, and more. Dementia damages these parts, making it hard for them to work together.

Effects on the Brain:

- **Memory Loss**: People may forget recent events or important information.
- **Trouble with Language**: Finding the right words or understanding others can be difficult.
- **Confusion**: They might be unsure about time or place.
- **Difficulty Thinking**: Solving problems or making decisions becomes harder.

Effects on the Body:

- **Movement Problems**: Some types of dementia affect balance and coordination.
- **Sleep Changes**: People might sleep more during the day and less at night.
- **Mood Swings**: Feelings can change quickly, from happy to sad or angry.

Understanding these effects helps us provide better care and support.

Types of Dementia

There are several types of dementia. Here are some common ones:

Alzheimer's Disease

- **What It Is**: The most common type of dementia.
- **Symptoms**: Starts with memory loss and can affect thinking and behavior.
- **Features**: Changes in the brain damage cells.

Vascular Dementia

- **What It Is**: Caused by reduced blood flow to the brain.
- **Symptoms**: Problems with planning, judgment, and movement.
- **Features**: Often linked to strokes or blood vessel issues.

Lewy Body Dementia

- **What It Is**: Involves unusual proteins in the brain.
- **Symptoms**: Memory loss, visual hallucinations, and movement difficulties.
- **Features**: Shares symptoms with Alzheimer's and Parkinson's disease.

Frontotemporal Dementia

- **What It Is**: Affects the front and side parts of the brain.
- **Symptoms**: Changes in personality, behavior, and language.
- **Features**: Often occurs in people between ages 40 and 65.

Each type affects people differently. Knowing the specific type can help in choosing the best care and support.

Why Early Detection Is Important

Finding out about dementia early can make a big difference. Here's why:

- **Access to Treatments**: Some medicines and therapies work best when started early.
- **Planning Ahead**: Early diagnosis allows time to make important decisions about care and finances.
- **Support Networks**: Families can find resources and support groups sooner.
- **Improving Quality of Life**: Early help can slow symptoms and keep the person active.

If you notice signs like memory loss or confusion, it's important to see a doctor. Early detection helps everyone prepare and ensures the person with dementia gets the support they need.

Chapter 2

Recognizing the Early Signs and Taking Action

Recognizing the early signs of dementia is important because it allows for timely action and support. In the beginning, dementia can be hard to notice. The changes might seem like normal aging or simple forgetfulness. However, certain signs can suggest that something more serious is happening.

One common early sign is memory loss. This isn't just occasionally forgetting where you left your keys. It's more serious and happens more often. A person might forget important dates or events. They might ask the same questions repeatedly, even after getting an answer. They might rely more on notes or family members to remember things they used to handle on their own.

Another sign is difficulty with familiar tasks. Everyday activities that used to be easy become hard. For example, cooking a favorite meal might become confusing. Following a recipe or remembering how to make a simple dish can be challenging. Driving to familiar places might become difficult, and they might get lost on the way to the store or a friend's house.

Problems with language can also be an early sign. Someone may struggle to find the correct words. They might stop in the middle of a conversation and not know how to continue. They might call things by the wrong name, like calling a watch a "**hand clock**."

Confusion about time and place is another warning sign. They may become confused about their location or how they arrived there. Understanding something that isn't happening right now can be hard. Dates, seasons, and the passage of time might become confusing. They might forget where they are, even in familiar settings.

Poor judgment is also a concern. They might make decisions that seem unusual or unsafe. For example, they might give large amounts of money to strangers. They may become less attentive to personal grooming or maintaining cleanliness.

Changes in mood or personality can occur. They might become confused, suspicious, depressed, or anxious. They might get upset easily, especially when they are out of their comfort zone. They might lose interest in activities they used to enjoy.

It's important to understand the difference between normal aging and dementia. As people get older, they might forget a name but remember it later. They might make a mistake balancing a checkbook but correct it the next time. They might sometimes feel tired of work or social obligations.

In dementia, the changes are more serious and happen more often. Memory loss disrupts daily life. They might forget important dates or events and not remember them later. They might need help from family members with things they used to do on their own.

If you observe these signs in yourself or a loved one, it's crucial to take steps right away. Start by writing down what you've noticed. Keep track of the changes and how often they happen. This information will be helpful when talking to a doctor.

Having a gentle conversation with your loved one is a good next step. Choose a time when you both are calm and won't be interrupted. Explain what you've noticed using kind words. For example, you might say, "**I've seen that you've been forgetting things more often lately. How do you feel about that?**" Listen carefully to their response.

Encourage them to see a doctor. Offer to help make the appointment and go with them. A doctor can check for other possible causes of the symptoms, like side effects from medicines or other health problems. Early detection can lead to better care and more options for treatment.

Preparing for the doctor's visit can make it more effective. Bring your notes about the symptoms you've observed. Make a list of all medicines being taken, including vitamins and supplements. Be ready to share any family history of dementia or other illnesses.

After seeing the doctor, if dementia is diagnosed, there are important steps to take. Learning about the type of dementia helps you know what to expect. Understanding the condition can reduce fear and confusion. Ask the doctor about ways to manage symptoms. Some treatments might help slow down changes or improve quality of life.

Planning for the future is important. Talk about legal and financial matters while your loved one can still share their wishes. This might include setting up a power of attorney, writing a will, or making plans for care needs. Having these discussions early can make things easier later on.

Building a support network is helpful. Connect with family, friends, and support groups. Sharing experiences with others can provide comfort and practical advice. There are many resources available for people with dementia and their caregivers.

Taking care of yourself is also important. Caring for someone with dementia can be challenging. Remember to take time for yourself and enjoy activities you love. Staying healthy helps you be a better caregiver.

It's normal to feel a range of emotions when dealing with dementia. You might feel sad, angry, or overwhelmed. Talking to a counselor or joining a support group can help you cope with these feelings.

Remember that your loved one is still the same person, even if they are changing. Focus on what they can do, not just on what they can't. Enjoy activities together that they still find meaningful. Simple pleasures like listening to music, looking at photos, or taking walks can bring joy.

Communication might become more challenging, but there are ways to stay connected. Use short, simple sentences. Speak slowly and clearly. Be patient and give them time to respond. Pay attention to body language and facial expressions. Creating a safe environment is important. Remove hazards like loose rugs or clutter that could cause falls. Make sure lighting is good throughout the house. Consider labeling cabinets and drawers to help them find things.

Establishing routines can provide comfort and reduce confusion. Keeping regular times for meals, activities, and bedtime helps them know what to expect. Familiarity can make them feel more secure.

It's also important to watch for changes in their health. Regular check-ups with the doctor can catch other problems early. Be alert for signs of pain, illness, or discomfort that they might not express.

Planning enjoyable activities can improve their quality of life. Adapt hobbies they used to enjoy to match their current abilities. For example, if they liked gardening, they might enjoy planting flowers in pots. If they liked cooking, they might help with simple tasks in the kitchen.

Involving them in social activities can help prevent feelings of isolation. Spending time with family and friends can lift their mood. Be mindful of their comfort level and adjust activities as needed.

Be patient with yourself and your loved one. There will be good days and bad days. Celebrate small successes and don't be too hard on yourself when things are tough. Keep in mind that you're giving your best effort in a challenging situation.

Reaching out for professional help when necessary shows strength. There are many services available, like home care aides, respite care, and counseling. Don't hesitate to reach out for assistance.

Understanding and recognizing the early signs of dementia allows you to take important steps. By acting early, you can access treatments, plan for the future, and find support.

This can make a significant difference in the lives of both you and your loved one.

Remember that you are not alone. Many families are going through similar experiences. By connecting with others and using available resources, you can navigate this journey with compassion and hope.

Chapter 3

Types of Dementia

Breaking Down the Variations

Dementia is not just one illness; it's a term that covers many different diseases that affect the brain. Each type of dementia changes the brain in its own way, leading to different symptoms and challenges. Knowing the specific type of dementia your loved one has can help you understand what they are going through and how best to support them.

The most common type of dementia is **Alzheimer's disease**. This disease affects memory, thinking, and behavior. In the beginning, a person might forget recent conversations or the names of familiar people and places. They might ask the same questions over and over. As time goes on, they may become confused about where they are or what day it is. Making decisions can become hard, and they might need help with daily tasks like cooking or getting dressed. Alzheimer's changes the brain by causing harmful proteins to build up, which damages brain cells and makes them die.

Another type is **vascular dementia**, which happens when the brain doesn't get enough blood flow. This can occur after a stroke or if blood vessels in the brain are blocked or damaged. People with vascular dementia might have trouble planning, making decisions, or solving problems. They may think more slowly and have trouble organizing their thoughts. Sometimes, they might have weakness on one side of the body or problems with balance, leading to falls or clumsiness.

Lewy Body Dementia is less common but can be very challenging. It happens when unusual proteins, called Lewy bodies, build up in the brain cells. People with this type might have memory problems similar to Alzheimer's, but they also have other symptoms. They might see things that aren't there, known as visual hallucinations. Sleep problems are common, and they might act out their dreams while sleeping. Movement can be affected too, causing stiffness or shakiness, like in Parkinson's disease. Their abilities might change from day to day, sometimes being alert and other times confused.

Frontotemporal Dementia affects the front and sides of the brain, which control personality, behavior, and language. People with this type might start acting differently than they used to. They could become impulsive, say inappropriate things, or lose interest in activities they once enjoyed. Some might have trouble speaking or understanding others. This type often affects people at a younger age, sometimes in their 50s or 60s, which can be especially hard for families to understand.

Mixed dementia occurs when an individual has multiple types of dementia at the same time. The most common combination is Alzheimer's disease and vascular dementia. This means they might have symptoms of both types, like memory loss and trouble thinking or planning. Physical problems like weakness or balance issues can also happen. Having mixed dementia can make symptoms more severe and can make it harder to diagnose and treat.

Creutzfeldt-Jakob Disease (CJD) is a rare and fast-moving type of dementia caused by abnormal proteins in the brain called prions. This disease progresses quickly, often leading to severe symptoms within a year. People with CJD might have rapid memory loss, muscle stiffness, and trouble walking. They may also have vision problems or sudden jerky movements. There is no cure for CJD, and care focuses on making the person comfortable and supporting the family.

Each type of dementia affects people differently. For example, Alzheimer's often starts with memory problems, while vascular dementia might begin with difficulties in thinking and planning. Lewy Body Dementia includes symptoms like seeing things that aren't there and movement problems. Frontotemporal Dementia affects behavior and language more than memory at first.

Understanding these differences helps you provide the best care for your loved one. It allows you to prepare for the specific challenges that might come up. Knowing what to expect can make a difficult journey a bit easier. It also helps you communicate better with doctors and other caregivers, ensuring that your loved one gets the support they need.

Remember, each person with dementia is unique. They may not show all the typical symptoms of their type, and the disease can progress differently in each individual. Being patient, staying informed, and offering loving support are the most important things you can do. By learning about the specific type of dementia, you can find ways to connect with your loved one and help them live their life with dignity and comfort.

Chapter 4

Understanding Risk Factors and Preventive Measures

Taking care of our brain health is something we all can do. Even though some things that increase the risk of dementia are beyond our control, like getting older or the genes we inherit, there are many choices we can make to help keep our minds sharp. By focusing on what we can change, we can take real steps to lower the chances of developing dementia.

One of the most powerful tools we have is our **lifestyle**. How we live each day can make a big difference in how our brains work. Staying active helps not only our bodies but also our brains. When we move, we increase blood flow to the brain, which brings oxygen and nutrients that help it stay healthy.

Physical activity is very important. Activities like walking, dancing, riding a bike, swimming, or even gardening can be enjoyable ways to stay active. You don't need to be an athlete; just find activities you like and do them regularly. Even small amounts of exercise can make a difference. For example, if you have a pet dog, taking it for daily walks is a great way to stay active. If you enjoy music, putting on your favorite songs and dancing around the house can be both fun and good exercise. Physical activity doesn't have to be a chore; it can be something you look forward to each day.

What we eat also matters a lot. A **healthy diet** filled with fruits, vegetables, whole grains, lean proteins, and good fats like those in fish, nuts, and olive oil can help our brains stay strong. These foods provide vitamins and minerals that support brain function. On the other hand, eating too many processed foods, sugary snacks, or unhealthy fats might increase the risk of memory problems.

You might start by adding more colorful fruits and vegetables to your meals. For breakfast, you could have oatmeal topped with berries and a sprinkle of nuts. For lunch, a salad loaded with different veggies and a light dressing can be both tasty and healthy. For dinner, choosing grilled fish or chicken with steamed vegetables and brown rice provides a balanced meal. Snacking on fruits, yogurt, or a handful of nuts instead of chips or cookies can make a positive difference.

Keeping our minds busy is important too. Doing mental activities like reading books, solving puzzles, playing board games, or learning new skills keeps the brain active. When we challenge our brains, we help them build new connections, which can keep them strong. For instance, you might join a book club where you can read and discuss books with others. This not only keeps your mind engaged but also provides social interaction. Learning a new language or taking up a musical instrument are great ways to challenge your brain.

Social interactions are also very helpful. Spending time with friends and family can boost our mood and support brain health. Talking, laughing, and sharing experiences with others can make us feel connected and happy. Consider setting regular times to meet with friends, whether it's a weekly coffee date or a monthly game night. Volunteering is another way to stay social and give back to the community. Participating in group activities like exercise classes, art workshops, or choir groups can combine socializing with other healthy habits.

Managing stress is another important factor. Stress can affect the brain in negative ways. Finding ways to relax can help. One method is practicing mindfulness, which means focusing on the present moment. This can be as simple as paying attention to your breathing or noticing the sights and sounds around you during a walk. Engaging in creative activities like painting, drawing, knitting, or writing can be relaxing and give you a sense of accomplishment.

Getting enough sleep is vital for brain health. During sleep, our brains get the opportunity to rest and heal. Lack of quality sleep can raise the risk of memory issues. To improve sleep, try to keep a regular schedule by going to bed and waking up at the same time each day, even on weekends. Create a relaxing bedtime routine, such as taking a warm bath, reading a book, or listening to soft music. Make sure your bedroom is comfortable, with a supportive mattress and pillows, and keep the room dark and quiet.

Taking care of our heart health is also linked to brain health. The brain needs a healthy heart to supply it with blood. Keeping blood pressure, cholesterol, and blood sugar levels in check can reduce the risk of conditions that may lead to dementia, like strokes or heart disease. Following a heart-healthy diet, staying active, and not smoking are key steps. If you have conditions like diabetes or high blood pressure, working with your doctor to manage them is important.

While we can control many things, there are some risk factors we can't change. As we get older, the risk of dementia increases. This doesn't mean everyone will develop it, but age is a factor we can't avoid. Our genes also play a role. If someone in our family has had dementia, our risk might be higher. But even then, it doesn't mean we will definitely get it.

Some health conditions, like diabetes, high blood pressure, or high cholesterol, can increase the risk of dementia. While we might not be able to change the fact that we have these conditions, we can manage them with the help of doctors and healthy habits. Regular check-ups and following treatment plans are important steps.

Knowing about these risks helps us focus on what we can do to help ourselves. By making healthy choices, we can take steps to protect our brains. Even small changes can add up over time.

Let's talk more about how to incorporate these brain-healthy habits into our daily lives. It might seem hard at first, but starting with small steps can make it easier.

For example, when it comes to diet, you don't have to change everything at once. You might begin by including an additional serving of vegetables in your meals. Maybe try a new fruit each week. Swapping white bread for whole-grain bread or choosing water instead of sugary drinks are simple changes that can make a difference. Cooking meals at home instead of eating out can also help you make healthier choices.

With physical activity, find things you enjoy. If you like music, maybe try dancing. If you enjoy nature, go for walks in the park. You can invite friends to join you, making it a social activity too. Setting small goals, like walking for 15 minutes a day, can help you get started. Over time, you can increase your activity as you feel comfortable.

To keep your mind active, think about what interests you. If you like reading, visit the library and find new books. If you're curious about a topic, look for documentaries or take an online class. Playing games that challenge your brain, like crossword puzzles or sudoku, can be both fun and beneficial. Trying new things keeps your mind engaged.

Staying connected with others is important. You can schedule regular phone calls or video chats with friends and family. Joining local groups or clubs can help you meet new people. Volunteering for a cause you care about is another way to connect with others and contribute to your community.

Managing stress can be as simple as taking a few minutes each day to relax. You might start by practicing deep breathing exercises. Sit in a comfortable position, close your eyes, and breathe deeply and slowly. Concentrate on the sensation of the air as it enters and exits your body. This can help soothe both your mind and body. Engaging in activities that bring you joy can also reduce stress.

Improving sleep habits can start with creating a calming bedtime routine. Perhaps enjoy a warm cup of herbal tea before bed. Reading a book or writing in a journal can help you unwind. Avoiding caffeine or heavy meals close to bedtime can also help. If you find that worries keep you awake, you might try writing down your thoughts before bed.

Taking care of your heart health might involve simple changes like reducing salt intake, choosing healthier fats, and eating more fiber-rich foods. Regular physical activity helps too. If you're a smoker, seeking help to quit can greatly improve heart and brain health.

Remember, it's okay to start small. Making one change at a time can lead to big results over time. Celebrate your successes, no matter how small they seem. Every positive step you take is important.

It's also helpful to involve others. Friends and family can support you in making healthy changes. You might find a walking buddy or share healthy recipes with each other. Encouraging each other can make the journey more enjoyable.

While we can't change our age or genes, focusing on these lifestyle changes gives us some control over our brain health. It's empowering to know that our choices can make a difference.

Taking care of ourselves is a journey that lasts a lifetime. By making healthy habits part of our daily lives, we can work towards reducing the risk of dementia and improving our overall well-being. It's about making choices each day that support our minds and bodies.

Every positive action we take today can help us enjoy a healthier tomorrow. Let's embrace these habits and take steps towards a brighter future.

Chapter 5

The Stages of Dementia – What to Expect

Dementia is a journey that unfolds over time, and knowing what to expect can help you support your loved one. Understanding the stages of dementia can make it easier to provide the right care when it's needed.

Dementia usually progresses through three stages: early, middle, and late. Each stage brings different changes and challenges.

In the early stage, the signs of dementia might be easy to miss. Your loved one may forget recent events or struggle to find the right words. They might misplace things more often or have trouble with tasks like paying bills or planning activities. They may still do most things on their own but might need a little help with some tasks. They might feel frustrated or embarrassed by these changes.

As dementia moves into the middle stage, the changes become more noticeable. Memory problems get worse, and your loved one might forget important information like their address or family members' names. They might have trouble following conversations or instructions. They may become confused about where they are or what day it is. Changes in mood and behavior can happen, such as becoming anxious, upset, or wandering away from home. They will need more help with daily tasks like cooking, dressing, or taking medicine.

In the late stage, dementia affects almost every part of your loved one's life. They may not recognize familiar people or remember their own past. Communication becomes very limited. They might have trouble eating, walking, or even sitting up. They will need help with all daily activities. Keeping them comfortable and safe becomes the main focus.

Throughout these stages, your care and support will need to change to meet their needs.

In the early stage, you can help by:

- **Creating routines**: Having a regular schedule can reduce confusion.
- **Using reminders**: Calendars, notes, or alarms can help them remember important things.
- **Encouraging independence**: Let them do as much as they can on their own, offering help when needed.
- **Being patient**: Give them time to find words or complete tasks.

In the middle stage, you might need to:

- **Simplify tasks**: Break activities into small steps.
- **Provide more assistance**: Help with daily tasks like cooking, cleaning, and personal care.
- **Ensure safety**: Remove tripping hazards, install grab bars, and keep an eye on them to prevent wandering.
- **Communicate clearly**: Use simple sentences and speak slowly.

In the late stage, focus on:

- **Providing comfort**: Make sure they are physically comfortable and manage any pain.
- **Offering gentle care**: Assist with eating, bathing, and dressing.
- **Using non-verbal communication**: A smile, a gentle touch, or soothing words can show love and reassurance.
- **Creating a calm environment**: Keep noise levels low and surroundings familiar.

Here are some practical tips to help you along the way:

- **Stay flexible**: Be ready to adjust routines as their needs change.
- **Seek support**: Don't hesitate to ask for help from family, friends, or professionals.
- **Take care of yourself**: Caring for someone with dementia can be stressful. Make sure to rest and do things you enjoy.
- **Stay connected**: Keep your loved one engaged with activities they enjoy, like listening to music or looking at photos.
- **Be patient and compassionate**: Remember that the changes are due to the illness, and your kindness makes a big difference.

Understanding the stages of dementia helps you prepare for what's ahead. By adapting your care to meet your loved one's changing needs, you can provide support, comfort, and love throughout their journey.

Chapter 6

The D.I.C.E. Approach – Managing Behavioral Changes

Caring for someone with dementia can bring challenges, especially when they show behaviors like anger, confusion, or wandering. The D.I.C.E. approach is a helpful way to understand and manage these behaviors. D.I.C.E. stands for Describe, Investigate, Create, and Evaluate. It gives you steps to follow to make things better for both you and your loved one.

First, **Describe** what's happening. When your loved one shows a challenging behavior, take note of the details. What time did it happen? What were they doing? Who was there? For example, if they become upset during bath time, notice what might be causing it. Maybe the water is too hot, or they feel embarrassed.

Next, **Investigate** why the behavior is happening. Think about possible reasons. Are they in pain? Are they hungry or thirsty? Are they feeling lonely or scared? Sometimes, people with dementia can't tell us what they need, so we have to look for clues. If they are restless, maybe they need to use the bathroom or are uncomfortable in their clothes.

Then, **Create** a plan to help. Based on what you've learned, think of ways to make things better. If bath time is upsetting, maybe a sponge bath would be more comfortable. If they become angry in noisy places, try keeping the environment quiet and calm. The plan should be simple and focused on their needs.

Finally, **Evaluate** how the plan is working. Watch to see if the behavior improves. If things get better, that's great! If not, you might need to try something different. It's okay to adjust your plan until you find what works best.

Let's look at some common behaviors and how the **D.I.C.E.** approach can help.

Aggression can be scary and hard to handle. If your loved one is acting out, start by describing when and where it happens. Investigate possible causes like pain, frustration, or feeling rushed. Create a calmer environment or give them more time to do things. Evaluate if these changes help reduce their anger.

Confusion is another common issue. Your loved one might not recognize familiar places or people. Describe the situations when they seem most confused. Investigate if changes in routine or surroundings might be causing it. Create a consistent daily schedule and keep their environment familiar. Evaluate if this helps them feel more secure.

Wandering can be dangerous. They might leave the house and get lost. Describe when they tend to wander. Investigate if they are bored, anxious, or looking for something. Create safe ways for them to move around, like setting up a walking path in the yard. Use locks or alarms to keep them safe. Evaluate if these steps reduce wandering.

The **D.I.C.E.** approach isn't just for problems—it can also help create positive moments. For example, if getting dressed is stressful, describe what's difficult for them. Investigate if they dislike certain clothes or feel overwhelmed by choices. Create a simple system by laying out two outfit choices. Make the environment calm and unhurried. Evaluate if this makes dressing easier and more pleasant.

During mealtimes, if they aren't eating well, describe their behavior. Investigate if they have trouble chewing or don't like certain foods. Create meals with easy-to-eat foods they enjoy. Make the dining area peaceful. Evaluate if their appetite improves.

Conversations can also be more enjoyable with **D.I.C.E.** Describe how they respond when you talk with them. Investigate topics they like or times of day they're more alert. Create conversations around happy memories or favorite subjects. Keep distractions low. Evaluate if they engage more.

By using the **D.I.C.E.** approach, you can better understand your loved one's needs and make caring for them a bit easier. Remember to be patient and kind, both to them and yourself. It's okay to ask for help and to try different things until you find what works. Caring for someone with dementia is a journey, and tools like **D.I.C.E.** can help make that journey smoother and more meaningful.

Chapter 7

Care and Treatment Options
Making Informed Decisions

Caring for a loved one with dementia involves making many important decisions about their treatment and care. Understanding the options can help you feel more confident and less overwhelmed. There are different treatments available, including medical treatments, alternative therapies, and long-term care choices.

Medical Treatments

Medical treatments for dementia aim to manage symptoms and improve quality of life. While there is no cure for dementia, certain medicines can help with memory loss, confusion, and mood changes.

Doctors may prescribe medicines that help improve memory and thinking. Some medicines work by boosting chemicals in the brain that help with memory and learning. Others help control brain chemicals to improve daily functioning. These medicines may not stop the disease from progressing, but they can help maintain abilities for a longer time.

Sometimes, doctors also prescribe medicines to help with other symptoms like depression, anxiety, or sleep problems. Treating these symptoms can improve overall well-being.

Researchers are working on new treatments that may help more in the future. Some of these include therapies that aim to remove harmful proteins in the brain or use gentle electrical stimulation to improve brain activity. While these are still being studied, they offer hope for better treatments down the road.

Alternative Therapies

In addition to medical treatments, alternative therapies can support a person with dementia. These focus on overall well-being and can complement medical care.

Exercise is very helpful. Regular physical activity can improve mood, maintain strength and balance, and even help with thinking skills. Activities like walking, swimming, or gentle stretching can be enjoyable and beneficial.

A healthy diet supports brain health. Eating plenty of fruits, vegetables, whole grains, lean proteins, and healthy fats like those found in fish and nuts can be good for the brain. Drinking enough water is also important.

Keeping the mind active with mental activities can help maintain thinking skills. Activities like puzzles, memory games, or learning new things can stimulate the brain. Participating in social activities and staying connected with others can also improve mood and cognitive function.

Long-Term Care Options

As dementia progresses, the level of care needed changes. Deciding on long-term care options can be challenging, but understanding them can help you make the best choice for your loved one.

Home Care

Many families start with home care, allowing the person to stay in familiar surroundings. Care can be given by family members, friends, or professional caregivers who visit the home. Home care can include help with daily tasks like cooking, cleaning, bathing, and taking medicine.

Home care works well in the early stages of dementia when symptoms are mild. As the disease progresses, the person may need more support than can be provided at home.

Assisted Living

Assisted living facilities offer more structured support. They provide a safe environment with staff available to help with daily activities. Residents usually have their own rooms or apartments and can participate in social and recreational activities.

Some assisted living facilities have special memory care units designed for people with dementia. These units have staff trained to meet the specific needs of those with memory loss. Moving to assisted living is often considered when safety becomes a concern or when the person needs more help than can be provided at home.

Hospice Care

Hospice care focuses on comfort and quality of life in the final stages of dementia. It provides support for both the person with dementia and their family. Hospice care can be offered at home, in a hospice facility, or in a nursing home.

Hospice care teams include doctors, nurses, social workers, and spiritual advisors who work together to manage pain and other symptoms and to provide emotional support.

Making the Decision

Deciding on long-term care involves considering the person's needs, safety, and preferences, as well as the family's ability to provide care. It's important to involve healthcare professionals in the decision-making process. They can provide guidance and help assess when it's time to consider different care options.

Questions to Ask Healthcare Providers and Care Facilities

When exploring care options, asking the right questions can help you make informed decisions. Here are some important questions to consider:

About Medical Care:

- What experience does the staff have in caring for people with dementia?
- Are medical professionals available when needed?
- How are emergencies handled?
- How is medicine managed?

About Daily Life:

- What is the daily routine like?
- What activities are offered?
- How are residents encouraged to participate?
- Is help available for those with mobility issues?

About Family Involvement:

- How will we be updated on our loved one's condition?
- Can we be involved in care planning?
- What are the visiting policies?

About Costs:

- What are the costs, and what services are included?
- Are there payment plans or financial assistance available?

About the Environment:

- What safety measures are in place?
- Is the facility clean and well-maintained?
- How does the staff interact with residents?
- Are there outdoor spaces and quiet areas?

Asking these questions can help you choose a care option that meets your loved one's needs and provides peace of mind for your family.

Making decisions about care and treatment options for a loved one with dementia can be difficult, but understanding the available options can make it easier. By learning about medical treatments, alternative therapies, and long-term care choices, you can make informed decisions that improve quality of life. Remember to seek support from healthcare professionals, ask questions, and take it one step at a time. You're not alone on this journey, and there are resources and people ready to help.

Chapter 8

Taking Care of the Caregiver – You Matter Too

Caring for a loved one with dementia is a generous and loving act, but it can also be very hard on you. It's essential to remember that your well-being is equally important. Taking care of yourself isn't selfish—it's necessary. When you feel good, you're better able to care for your loved one.

Being a caregiver can be exhausting, both physically and emotionally. You might feel tired all the time, stressed out, or even burned out. These feelings can build up slowly, and sometimes you might not notice them right away. It's important to recognize the signs that you might need a break.

You might find yourself feeling very tired, even after you rest. Little things might start to bother you more than they used to. You might feel sad, guilty, or helpless. You might stop enjoying activities you used to love, or you might pull away from friends and family. You might also neglect your own needs, like skipping meals or not getting enough sleep.

If you're feeling this way, remember you're not alone, and it's perfectly fine to seek help. Looking after yourself enables you to better care for your loved one.

Practical Tips for Taking Care of Yourself

One of the most important things you can do is to take breaks. It might feel like you need to be there all the time, but everyone needs rest. Even short breaks during the day can help. Take a few minutes to sit quietly, take deep breaths, or enjoy a cup of tea. These small moments can refresh your mind and body.

Try to plan longer breaks when you can. Maybe a friend or family member can stay with your loved one for a few hours while you rest, run errands, or do something you enjoy. If possible, consider hiring a professional caregiver for a few hours or days to give you more time to recharge.

Don't be afraid to ask for help. Friends and family often want to help but might not know how. Let them know what you need. Maybe someone can help with shopping, cooking, or just spending time with your loved one so you can rest. Remember, asking for help isn't a sign of weakness—it's a way to make sure both you and your loved one are cared for.

Setting boundaries is also important. It's alright to decline additional tasks if you're feeling overwhelmed. Try to set aside time each day just for yourself, even if it's only a few minutes. Use this time to do something that makes you happy, like reading, taking a walk, or listening to music.

Finding Support

You don't have to go through this alone. Connecting with others can make a big difference. Joining a caregiver support group can provide comfort and understanding. In these groups, you can share your feelings and experiences with people who understand what you're going through. They can offer advice, support, and friendship.

Support groups can be found in your community or online. Online groups can be especially helpful if you can't leave the house easily. Talking to others can help you feel less isolated and provide new ideas for coping with challenges.

Consider talking to a counselor or therapist. They can provide a safe space to express your feelings and help you find ways to manage stress. They can also offer strategies to cope with difficult emotions like guilt, anger, or sadness.

Taking Care of Your Health

Your health matters. When you take care of your own physical and mental health, you're better able to care for your loved one. Make time for activities that boost your mood and energy. Regular physical activity, like walking or gentle stretching, can help reduce stress and improve your mood. Even short periods of activity can make a difference.

Eat regular, healthy meals. It might be tempting to skip meals when you're busy, but your body needs fuel. Try to include fruits, vegetables, whole grains, and lean proteins in your diet. Staying hydrated is important, too.

Sleep is essential. Aim for enough rest each night. If you’re struggling with sleep, consider creating a calming bedtime routine. If you can't get a full night's sleep, short naps during the day can help.

Pay attention to your mental health. It's normal to feel a range of emotions. Allow yourself to feel them without judgment. Practices like deep breathing, meditation, or even spending a few quiet moments alone can help reduce stress.

Remember, it's okay to take time for yourself. Doing so doesn't mean you're neglecting your loved one. In fact, taking care of yourself means you'll have more patience and energy to care for them.

Balancing Caregiving and Self-Care

Finding a balance between caring for your loved one and caring for yourself can be challenging, but it's important. Here are some ideas to help:

- **Prioritize Tasks**: Focus on what's most important each day. It's okay if everything doesn't get done.
- **Be Kind to Yourself**: Recognize that you're doing the best you can. It's okay to have tough days.
- **Stay Connected**: Keep in touch with friends and family. A phone call or visit can boost your spirits.
- **Set Realistic Goals**: Recognize your limits and avoid taking on more than you can manage.
- **Celebrate Small Victories**: Acknowledge the small successes each day, both yours and your loved one's.

You Matter Too

Caring for someone with dementia is a big responsibility, but it shouldn't come at the expense of your own well-being. By taking care of yourself, you're not only helping yourself but also improving the care you provide.

Remember, you don't have to do this alone. Reach out for support when you need it. Taking care of yourself is one of the most important things you can do—for both you and your loved one.

Chapter 9

Navigating Legal and Financial Challenges

Facing a diagnosis of dementia can be overwhelming, not just emotionally but also in terms of planning for the future. Taking care of legal and financial matters early on can bring peace of mind and protect both your loved one and your family. It's important to address these issues while your loved one can still express their wishes clearly.

One of the first things to consider is creating a will. A will is a document that says what should happen to a person's belongings and assets after they pass away. This includes things like property, money, and personal items. Having a will ensures that their wishes are followed and can prevent disagreements among family members later on. If your loved one already has a will, it's a good idea to review it regularly to make sure it reflects their current wishes and any changes in their life.

Another important step is setting up a power of attorney. This is a legal document that allows someone your loved one trusts to make decisions on their behalf if they are no longer able to do so.

There are two main types:

- **Financial Power of Attorney**: This person can manage financial matters like paying bills, handling bank accounts, and taking care of property.
- **Healthcare Power of Attorney**: This person can make medical decisions, such as treatments and care options.

Having a power of attorney in place ensures that someone is ready to step in and help when needed, without delays or legal hurdles.

In some cases, if no power of attorney is set up and your loved one can no longer make decisions, the court may appoint a guardian to make decisions for them. This process can be lengthy and stressful, so it's better to plan ahead with a power of attorney.

Planning for the financial aspects of dementia care is also important. Care can be expensive, and costs can add up over time. Understanding what resources are available can help ease the burden.

First, review any health insurance coverage your loved one has. Medicare is a federal program that helps with medical costs for people over 65, but it may not cover long-term care like nursing homes or in-home care. Medicaid is a program that can help with these costs for people with limited income and resources, but there are specific eligibility requirements.

Long-term care insurance is another option. This type of insurance can help pay for services like in-home care, assisted living, or nursing homes. However, it usually needs to be purchased before a dementia diagnosis, as it may be difficult or more expensive to get coverage afterward.

Costs for care can vary widely depending on the level of support needed:

- **In-home care**: Professional caregivers come to the home to help with daily tasks.

- **Assisted living facilities**: Provide housing and support for people who need help with daily activities but don't require constant medical care.
- **Nursing homes**: Offer 24-hour care and medical attention for those who need a higher level of support.

It's important to plan for these expenses and explore all options. Some families may also consider other resources, such as veterans' benefits for those who have served in the military, or using life insurance policies that allow for early payouts.

To help manage these financial decisions, consider consulting a financial planner who specializes in elder care. They can help create a plan that fits your loved one's needs and resources.

Planning for the future also includes managing your loved one's estate. This means organizing their assets and ensuring their wishes are followed. Besides having a will and power of attorney, here are some steps to consider:

- **Set up a living trust**: This is a way to manage assets during your loved one's lifetime and distribute them after they pass away, often avoiding the need for court processes.
- **Create advance directives**: These are written instructions about the kind of medical care your loved one wants if they are unable to communicate. This can include preferences about life support or other treatments.
- **Review beneficiary designations**: Check accounts like life insurance policies and retirement funds to make sure the right people are listed to receive these assets.

- **Plan for taxes**: Some assets may have tax implications for those who inherit them. Consulting a tax advisor can help minimize any unexpected taxes.

Working with an elder law attorney can ensure all legal documents are properly prepared and up to date. They can help navigate complex laws and make sure your loved one's rights and wishes are protected.

To keep everything organized, it's helpful to create a checklist of important documents and steps:

1. **Will**: Ensure it's current and reflects your loved one's wishes.
2. **Power of Attorney**: Set up both financial and healthcare powers of attorney.
3. **Advance Directives**: Document medical care preferences.
4. **Living Trust**: Consider if this is right for your loved one's situation.
5. **Financial Inventory**: Make a list of all accounts, assets, and debts.
6. **Beneficiary Designations**: Review and update as needed.
7. **Insurance Policies**: Understand what coverage is in place.
8. **Long-Term Care Planning**: Research options and costs for different care levels.
9. **Document Organization**: Keep all important documents in a safe, accessible place.
10. **Regular Reviews**: Update documents and plans as circumstances change.

By taking these steps, you can help ensure that your loved one's wishes are honored and that legal and financial matters are handled smoothly. Early planning can reduce stress and provide peace of mind for everyone involved.

Remember, you're not alone in this process. Professionals like attorneys, financial planners, and healthcare providers can offer guidance and support. Taking the time to address these challenges now can make a big difference in the future.

Chapter 10

Emotional Support and Communication for Families

Caring for a loved one with dementia brings many challenges, especially when it comes to communication. As the disease progresses, your loved one may have trouble remembering things, become confused, or struggle to find the right words. But even when communication becomes difficult, it's still possible to connect and share meaningful moments together.

Maintaining Communication

Being patient is one of the most important things you can do. Conversations may take longer, and your loved one might repeat themselves or have trouble following along. Allow them to express themselves at their own pace without hurrying or interrupting. Remember, the goal is to share time together, not to have a perfect conversation.

Using simple language can help. Speak in short sentences and use clear, straightforward words. Instead of asking open-ended questions like, "**What would you like for dinner**?" try offering specific choices: "Wo**uld you like chicken or fish for dinner?**" This makes it easier for them to understand and respond.

Non-verbal communication becomes more important as words become harder to find. A warm smile, a gentle touch, or eye contact can show your love and support. Sometimes, just sitting together quietly can be comforting.

Focus on their feelings rather than the exact words they use. If they seem upset or frustrated, acknowledge their emotions by saying things like, "**I can see you're feeling sad. I'm here with you.**" This shows that you care and helps them feel understood. Create a calm environment when you talk. Turn off the TV or move to a quiet space to reduce distractions. This helps your loved one focus better on the conversation.

Using memory aids like photo albums or familiar objects can spark conversations. Looking at old pictures together can bring back happy memories and give you something to talk about.

Stay positive during your time together. Laughter, shared smiles, or even comfortable silence can strengthen your connection. Accepting that things have changed can help you adapt your communication style and maintain your bond.

Preserving Dignity and Connection

As dementia progresses to later stages, your loved one may need more help with daily activities. It's important to support them in a way that respects their dignity.

Treat them with respect in all interactions. Speak to them as an adult, not as a child. Even if they can't respond, they may still understand more than you realize.

When helping with personal care like bathing or dressing, explain what you're doing. Offer choices when possible, like choosing between two outfits or asking if they'd prefer a bath or a shower. This helps them feel involved and maintains a sense of control.

Find new ways to connect. Music can be a powerful tool. Playing their favorite songs might bring joy and even encourage them to hum or sing along. Simple touches, like holding hands or giving a gentle hug, can also provide comfort.

Keep routines consistent. Having regular times for meals, activities, and rest can provide a sense of security. Familiar routines can help your loved one feel more at ease.

Instead of correcting them if they say something that's not accurate, gently go along with their reality when appropriate. This can reduce frustration and make interactions more peaceful.

Use sensory experiences to connect. Activities like brushing their hair, offering a soft blanket, or enjoying pleasant scents can provide comfort when words aren't enough.

Remember to be patient. Allow them to move at their own pace, and try not to rush through tasks. Your calm and understanding presence can make a big difference.

Talking to Children About Dementia

Children may notice changes in a family member with dementia and might feel confused or scared. It's important to talk to them openly and honestly.

Use simple language that's right for their age. You might say, "**Grandma is sick, and it's making it hard for her to remember things.**" Let them ask questions and answer them honestly.

Reassure them that it's not their fault and that they can't catch dementia like a cold. Encourage them to share their feelings and let them know it's okay to feel sad or upset.

Involve them in activities they can share with their loved one. Drawing pictures, playing simple games, or looking at photos together can help maintain a connection.

Prepare them for changes they might see. Explain that sometimes Grandma might forget their name or repeat herself, but she still loves them very much.

Let them know it's okay if things feel different or a little uncomfortable. Remind them that their love and time mean a lot.

Sharing Responsibilities and Seeking Support

Caring for someone with dementia can be overwhelming. It's important for family members to work together and share the responsibilities.

Have open conversations with your family about what needs to be done. Divide tasks based on each person's strengths and availability. One person might handle doctor appointments, another might manage finances, and others might help with daily care.

Don't hesitate to seek professional help. Hiring a caregiver or using respite care services can provide much-needed relief. This allows family members to rest and take care of their own well-being.

Support each other. Recognize when someone needs a break and offer to step in. Encourage one another to take time for self-care and to look after their own health.

Consider joining a support group. Connecting with others who are going through similar experiences can provide comfort and valuable advice.

Remember that dementia care is a journey that changes over time. Stay flexible and adapt as your loved one's needs evolve.

A Family's Journey

The Martinez family faced dementia when Maria, the grandmother, began showing signs of memory loss. Her children, Carla and Diego, and her husband, Antonio, noticed the changes and decided to get medical help.

They worked together to support Maria, involving her in decisions as much as possible. They kept communication simple and focused on spending quality time together. Gardening, which Maria loved, became a way for the family to connect and share happy moments.

As Maria's needs grew, they shared responsibilities. Antonio took care of her daily routines, Carla managed medical appointments and medications, and Diego handled finances and home repairs. They also hired a caregiver to help with personal care tasks.

Music played a big role in maintaining their connection. Playing Maria's favorite songs brought joy and often encouraged her to hum or tap along. They used photo albums to reminisce, helping Maria feel comforted by familiar faces and memories.

They explained the situation to Maria's grandchildren in simple terms, helping them understand and find ways to interact with her. Activities like drawing and looking at pictures allowed the children to bond with their grandmother.

The family held regular check-ins to support each other emotionally. They recognized the importance of self-care and encouraged one another to take breaks when needed.

By working together, seeking support, and focusing on emotional connections, the Martinez family navigated the challenges of dementia with love and resilience. Their journey shows how teamwork, flexibility, and staying connected can make a big difference.

Chapter 11

Resources and Support Networks

Caring for someone with dementia can be challenging, but you don't have to face it alone. Many organizations, groups, and tools are ready to support you and your loved one. By reaching out and connecting with these resources, you can find help, understanding, and a sense of community.

Finding Supportive Organizations

Several national and local organizations are dedicated to helping people affected by dementia. These groups offer information, services, and connections that can make a big difference in your caregiving journey.

One well-known organization is the Alzheimer's Association. Even though it focuses on Alzheimer's disease, it provides support for all types of dementia. They have a helpline you can call any time, day or night, to speak with trained professionals. This can be a lifeline during tough moments. The Alzheimer's Association also has local chapters across the country that host educational workshops, support groups, and community events. Attending these can help you learn more about dementia, meet others in similar situations, and feel less alone.

Another helpful resource is the Dementia Society of America. They offer programs and services for families and caregivers, providing educational materials to help you understand dementia better. They can connect you with local resources and activities that are friendly to people with dementia.

Your local Area Agency on Aging is also an important place to connect with. These agencies specialize in services for older adults, including those with dementia. They can help you find transportation services, meal delivery programs, and in-home care options. They offer information about legal and financial planning, which can be crucial as you navigate the complexities of dementia care.

If your loved one is a veteran, the Department of Veterans Affairs (VA) provides specialized support. The VA offers healthcare services, including memory care clinics and in-home support. They can assist with medical costs and connect you with other veterans experiencing similar challenges.

Local hospitals, clinics, and community health centers often have programs for people with dementia and their caregivers. They may offer classes on managing symptoms, advice on medications, and support groups. These resources can provide expert guidance and connect you with healthcare professionals who understand your situation.

Places of worship, like churches, synagogues, and mosques, may also offer support. Many have programs or outreach efforts aimed at helping families dealing with dementia. They can provide spiritual support, counseling, and community connections.

Joining Support Groups

Support groups can play a vital role in your journey. They offer a safe space to share feelings, learn from others, and find comfort. Both caregivers and people living with dementia can benefit greatly from participating in these groups.

Some support groups are designed specifically for caregivers, providing a place to discuss the stresses and joys of caring for someone with dementia. Talking about your experiences with others who understand can be deeply healing. You can learn practical tips, coping strategies, and feel validated in your feelings.

Other groups are tailored for individuals with dementia, especially those in the early stages. These groups allow them to connect with peers, share their experiences, and combat feelings of isolation.

Many organizations host support groups. The Alzheimer's Association, for instance, offers groups both in person and online. This flexibility means you can choose the option that best fits your schedule and comfort level. Online groups can be especially helpful if getting out of the house is a challenge or if you prefer the convenience of joining from home. Support groups offer more than just advice. They provide emotional support, friendship, and a sense of community. Knowing that others are facing similar challenges can reduce feelings of loneliness and anxiety.

Using Technology for Support

Technology has opened up new ways to find support and information. Online resources offer a wealth of knowledge and tools that can make caregiving more manageable.

Educational websites provide articles, videos, and webinars about dementia. These resources can help you understand the disease, its progression, and ways to care for your loved one.

Apps designed for caregivers can assist with organizing medications, appointments, and daily tasks. They offer features like reminders and shared calendars. This can help you stay organized and ensure important details are not overlooked.

For your loved one, there are apps and online activities that provide mental stimulation. Games that focus on memory or problem-solving can be both enjoyable and beneficial.

Communication tools are also valuable. Video chat apps enable you to connect with friends and family who may live far away. This can help your loved one stay socially engaged and feel connected to their wider community.

Safety is a crucial concern in dementia care. Technology can assist here too. GPS tracking devices or apps can help you keep track of your loved one's location, providing peace of mind. Medication management apps ensure that doses are not missed or duplicated.

Building a Support Network

Creating a network of support is essential for your well-being and that of your loved one. Don't hesitate to reach out to friends, family, and neighbors. People often want to help but may not know how. Let them know what would be useful, whether it's running errands, providing meals, or spending time with your loved one.

Consider setting up a schedule where different people assist at various times. This can lighten your load and provide variety for your loved one.

Professional caregivers can be an important part of your support network. Hiring in-home care services, even for a few hours a week, can give you much-needed rest. Respite care services offer temporary relief, allowing you to take a break, attend to personal matters, or simply rest.

Therapists and counselors can provide emotional support for both you and your loved one. Talking with a professional can help you process feelings, develop coping strategies, and navigate the emotional complexities of caregiving.

Legal and financial advisors who specialize in elder care can assist with planning for the future. They can help you understand options for care funding, estate planning, and legal documents like power of attorney.

Staying Informed and Engaged

Knowledge is a powerful tool in managing dementia care. Stay informed about the disease, treatments, and caregiving strategies. Attend workshops, read books, and participate in webinars.

Keep open communication with healthcare providers. Regular check-ups and honest discussions with doctors help ensure your loved one receives appropriate care. Don't hesitate to ask questions or express concerns.

Monitor changes in your loved one's condition. Noting shifts in behavior, mood, or abilities can help you address issues promptly.

Engaging with your community can enrich your caregiving experience. Participate in local events, activities, or programs designed for people with dementia and their families. These may include memory cafes, art classes, or music therapy sessions.

Practice self-compassion. Caring for someone with dementia can be demanding, and it's important to be kind to yourself. Take breaks when needed and engage in activities that nourish you.

You Are Not Alone

Remember that you are part of a larger community of people who understand what you're going through. By reaching out and connecting with others, you can find hope, encouragement, and practical help.

Embrace the support offered by organizations, groups, and individuals. Allow yourself to accept help and share your experiences. Together, you can face the challenges of dementia with resilience and compassion.

Your journey may be difficult at times, but you don't have to walk it alone. With the right resources and support networks, you can navigate this path more smoothly. You can find moments of joy, deepen your relationships, and create meaningful experiences along the way.

By staying connected, informed, and compassionate—both toward your loved one and yourself—you can make a positive difference in your lives. Help is available, and together, we can support each other through the journey of dementia.

Conclusion

Living with dementia or caring for someone who does is a journey that touches every part of life. It's filled with challenges, discoveries, and deep emotions. By recognizing this ongoing journey, we can face it with open hearts, ready to embrace both the difficult moments and the joys along the way.

Dementia brings changes that can be hard to navigate. Memory fades, familiar tasks become tricky, and conversations might get confusing. These changes are tough for everyone involved. It's normal to feel sad, frustrated, or overwhelmed. Acknowledging these feelings is an important step toward coping in a healthy way.

Understanding that dementia progresses over time helps set realistic expectations. There will be good days and hard days. Some moments may feel heavy, while others bring unexpected happiness. Embracing the journey means accepting these ups and downs and finding ways to adapt as needs change.

Caring for someone with dementia requires patience and kindness. Simple tasks might take longer, and conversations may need extra effort. By slowing down and focusing on the present moment, we can create meaningful interactions that honor the person's dignity and individuality. Celebrating small achievements and cherishing shared moments can bring comfort and strengthen your bond.

Remember, you're not alone. Many others are walking a similar path, facing similar feelings and uncertainties. This guide is here to support you whenever you need it, offering information, ideas, and encouragement. You can return to these pages as often as you like, finding reassurance and guidance along the way.

Connecting with others who understand your experiences can bring great comfort. Support groups, whether in person or online, offer spaces to share feelings, ask questions, and learn from others. Hearing about their journeys can provide new insights, practical tips, and a sense of belonging. It reminds us that we're part of a caring community.

Don't hesitate to reach out to professionals who can assist you. Doctors, counselors, and caregiving services are there to help. They can guide you through medical decisions, offer emotional support, and connect you with resources that fit your needs. Asking for help is a sign of strength and shows your commitment to providing the best care possible.

As you move forward, hold onto hope and embrace resilience. Hope isn't just about wishing for a cure; it's about finding meaning and joy in the journey itself. It's about recognizing the value of each moment and the strength that comes from facing challenges bravely. Resilience grows each time we overcome an obstacle or adapt to a new situation.

Lean on friends, family, and support networks. Share your stories and listen to theirs. Together, you can find creative solutions, celebrate successes, and offer comfort during tough times. Building a strong support system not only eases the burden but also enriches the journey with shared understanding and companionship.

Focusing on what remains rather than what's lost can make a significant difference. Treasure the smiles, the laughter, and the moments of connection. Engage in activities that bring joy and strengthen bonds, whether it's listening to music, looking at photos, or enjoying a simple walk together. These experiences nourish the spirit and deepen relationships.

Keep learning about dementia and caregiving. Knowledge empowers you to make informed decisions and adapt to changes. Stay curious and open to new information, and don't be afraid to ask questions. The more you know, the better prepared you'll be to navigate the journey.

Planning for the future is also important. Having open conversations about legal matters, financial planning, and care preferences can reduce uncertainty. While these talks might be difficult, they help ensure that your loved one's wishes are respected. Seeking professional advice can make this process smoother and provide peace of mind.

Recognize the growth and strength that have emerged throughout this journey. You've faced challenges with courage and compassion. You've adapted to new realities and found ways to maintain connection and love. These achievements are significant and deserve acknowledgment.

Continue to nurture yourself and your relationships. Practice self-care, understanding that it's okay to feel a range of emotions. Allow yourself to grieve losses but also to celebrate joys. Stay connected to your own interests and passions, as they provide balance and fulfillment.

Remember that love is at the heart of this journey. The care and support you provide are expressions of deep affection. This love sustains you and your loved one, creating a bond that endures through all challenges.

Every step you take on this path matters. Your efforts, kindness, and dedication make a profound difference. By embracing the challenges with understanding and reaching out for support when needed, you enhance the quality of life for your loved one and enrich your own.

Moving forward with strength and understanding is a continuous process. It's about finding balance, seeking joy in small moments, and nurturing the connections that give life meaning. With hope in your heart and a community by your side, you can navigate this journey with resilience and grace.

You are not alone, and together, we can make a positive difference in the lives of those affected by dementia. Hold onto hope, embrace the support around you, and continue forward with courage and compassion.

www.ingramcontent.com/pod-product-compliance
Lightning Source LLC
LaVergne TN
LVHW052034080726
842905LV00051B/1203
* 9 7 9 8 3 3 0 4 2 3 7 2 9 *